VIRTUOUS AND TEMPERATE

Women of Excellence

IN THE MODERN WORLD

Janice Mae Jackson

MANIFEST
PUBLICATIONS

ISBN: 978-1-951280-31-4

Names and references to God are capitalized to acknowledge and
worship His deity. In contrast, references to satan are not capitalized,
even to the point of violating grammatical rules, so as to equally
acknowledge his position of defeat.

Cover Design: Don Patton

Table of Contents

Introduction

We are living in a generation where women are displaying a lack of virtue. Many women are living in the ways of this world and not God's ways. Many women feel victimized and then act on their emotions out of desperation, and get themselves into situations that they never wanted to be in. They are hurting, they are living a life of brokenness with a broken Spirit, broken relationships, and broken self-esteem. But most of all a broken heart, which results in living a life of unforgiveness, bitterness, and anger.

Jesus tells us in His Word that His thoughts towards us are thoughts of peace and to give us a future and a hope. But before we can live in that state of peace and hope, there must be a change in our own lives. As women, we need to examine our lives, we need to understand why we are feeling and acting this way.

Do you want a high level of excellence in your life? This book is going to help you achieve a high level of excellence in your life. by helping you to understand that change is needed. This book will bring correction and give friendly advice and encouragement so that you can become a woman of excellence by becoming

1

virtuous and temperate.

This book will also reveal to you who your Heavenly Father is and how to come into right relationship with Him. And once you come into right relationship with God, you will know who you really are and you will be amazed by all He has made available to you for you to live an abundant life.

God, our Heavenly Father, wants to help us renew our minds through His Word. Why? Because real change starts with changing our minds and the way we think. This book will guide you through portions of God's Word to help you change the way you think so that your life can be set on the course of God's peace, abundance, and blessing.

This is my prayer for every woman reading this book.

Heavenly Father, I ask that you bless everyone who is reading this book right now in Jesus' name. Father God, it is not by accident that they are reading this book, but it is by Your design and purpose that You drew them to it.

Father, I ask that You open up their eyes and turn them from darkness to light and from the power of satan to You that they may receive forgiveness of sins through Jesus Christ. I ask that You remove the deafness from their ears so that they may hear what You are speaking to them in this season, and I ask that you open up their Spirit to receive the Word of God to allow change to come into their lives. I ask that You renew their minds so they can walk in victory and live their life in excellence in You.

Father, heal their hearts and lives of the pain and hurt that has come from every hurtful word spoken by anyone against them that pierced their heart, and wounded their soul. I ask that You remove the shackles of shame from their feet and set these captives free, because who the Son sets free is free indeed.

Father, I pray all of this in the mighty name of Jesus and seal this prayer with the blood of Jesus so that it cannot be broken.

Amen.

CHAPTER ONE
Titus 2: Women Who Are Virtuous & Temperate

In the book of Titus, Apostle Paul instructed a young pastor named Titus, who was pastoring a church in Crete, about how to organize the church. Titus was to be actively involved in instructing, encouraging, and teaching the godly older women so that they would be properly equipped for the task of leading the younger women.

Let's look at Titus Chapter 2.

Titus 2:3: *the older women likewise, that they be reverent in behavior, not slanderers, not given to much wine, teachers of good things--*
2:4 - that they admonish the young women to love their husbands, to love their children,
2:5 - [to be] discreet, chaste, homemakers, good, obedient to their own husbands, that the word of God may not be blasphemed.

Let's look at two important keys in verses 3 and 4.

Key words in these scriptures are that they:
1. Are teachers of good things.
2. Admonish the young women.

This is saying that older women are to assume the responsibilities of providing a proper example for women who are less mature on godly living, teaching them how to live self-controlled, exemplary, and fruitful lives.

Admonish: Bring correction whether, or if necessary, by reproof or encouragement.

Admonish[1]: to express warning or disapproval to, especially in a gentle earnest manner. (2) To give friendly earnest advice or encouragement.

Titus 2:12 - *teaching us that, denying ungodliness and worldly lusts, we should live soberly, righteously, and godly in the present age,*

Another word for sober is temperate which means self-control. We as women should act in a responsible manner by not acting out on our emotions but being in control of our emotions at all times, conducting ourselves properly.

---

[1] Merriam-Webster Dictionary

Sober: for which sober is translated Temperate

Temperate: Self-control

A primary role of a Christian leader is teaching. A godly woman should teach and train women to renounce godlessness and worldly pleasures; how to be temperate, exercising self-control, saying no to ungodly, worldly attitudes and behavior; and saying yes to righteous and godly living so they can live fruitful lives. The Word of God tells us that we should comfort each other and edify one another; edifying one another so we can help each other with spiritual growth and development of character by teaching or by example, therefore encouraging each other and building each other up.

CHAPTER TWO

Women Who Are Not Virtuous & Temperate

Over the years, I have seen women, even those who say that they are Christians, not being virtuous and temperate in their behavior. What is virtue? Below are three definitions of the word virtue, two from the Bible dictionary, and one from the world dictionary.

Virtue: Moral goodness; Excellencies

Virtue[2]: Moral excellency and goodness

Virtue[3]: Conformity to a standard of right, MORALITY, a particular moral excellence; Chastity especially in a woman.

While looking at many definitions of the word virtue, I came across an article that listed the definition of the word. The article did not have a title, nor did it state who it was written by, but out of all the

---

[2] Word Wealth, NKJV
[3] Merriam-Webster Dictionary

definitions I had read I really like this definition; this was the best definition that I have found that is closely related to the virtues that I am going to address to you. The article read:

> "What is the best definition of Virtue? Noun. Moral excellence: goodness, righteousness, conformity of one's life and conduct to moral and ethical principles, uprightness, rectitude, chastity."

All definitions define the word virtue as dealing with morals/moral excellencies; it is the moral excellence of a person. A morally excellent woman has a character that is made up of virtue valued as good. Virtues are the essence of our character, and character does determine destiny, and when we keep the practice of virtue at the heart of our everyday life, we live with purpose.

In my daily surroundings, wherever I go, I am always observing women:

1. How they carry themselves.
2. How they are dressed.
3. How they are treating their children.
4. What they are speaking out of their mouths to their children.
5. If they are being responsible and training their children.

6. How they are speaking to men.
7. How men are treating them.
8. Women chasing men.
9. How so many married women are heads of their household.

I am not only looking at women in my daily surroundings outside the church, but I am also looking at the women who proclaim they are believers, who proclaim to be daughters of the Most High God. It saddens me to see how women are acting in these times, what I see is a lack of virtue, women without virtue. This virtue is not only lacking among women who are still in the world, who have not yet given their lives to Christ, but it is very much lacking among women who are in the Church. What I see is that in each generation of women is that virtue declines.

There is a lack of moral conduct among women today, not just among women in the world, but also among Christian women. We have Christian women who look like, act like, and demonstrate all the facets of the world; and a lack of this morality is happening right inside the Church. Today you cannot tell the difference between the worldly women and the Christian women. Christian women have conformed themselves to the ways of the world and not God's ways. I have seen women who proclaim that they are Christians, women who are in the Church, and worldly women exhibiting the same behaviors in their lives. Things such as:

1. No morals.
2. No goodness.
3. Unrighteousness
4. Using profanity.
5. Lying.
6. Conformity to the world standards.
7. Lack of self-control.
8. No integrity.
9. Having no self-respect.
10. Exhibiting Provocativeness.
11. Chasing men.
12. Cursing children.
13. Neglecting their children.
14. No domestic skills.
15. Married and acting as head of household.
16. Women fighting over a male.
17. Fornication.
18. Adultery.
19. Living in sin.

This is what a lot of women are exhibiting in their lives, and we are not to be living our lives in this darkened lifestyle. You may say, "the men are doing many of the same things." And yes, I agree, but I am only addressing the women. Many women would say that society has changed so morality changed, and what seemed immoral a few years ago is considered and accepted as moral today. Society has changed but God's words have not changed and will not change. He has a standard that He requires of us, and that standard has not changed. Once we have the right standard, God's standard, then the image of the world that has been displayed in your life will be removed and the image of God will be displayed. God calls us to a higher standard because He has called us to be Christ-like. We are called to strip off our old nature (our former way of life) because our old nature is thoroughly rotten by its deceptive desires and we must clothe ourselves with the new nature created to be godly, putting Him first in our lives. God's Word tells us:

Romans 12:2 -*And do not be conformed to this world, but be transformed by the renewing of your mind, that you may prove what [is] that good and acceptable and perfect will of God.*

This scripture is giving us three important keys:
1. Do not be conformed to this world.
2. Transformation comes when your mind is renewed.
3. That you should be doing God's acceptable and perfect will.

We are living in a godless system, and we are not to

accept the patterns of this world whose god is satan who has blinded the minds of many women. The above scripture is saying not to let ourselves be conformed to the standards of this world, that we should not conform ourselves or our outward appearance, modeling ourselves to the ways of the world. When we model ourselves to the ways of the world, we are being contaminated by the world and we begin to desecrate the name of God by our actions. By doing so, we are representing the world not the Kingdom; we are representing satan, not Jesus. Jesus' name in Hebrew is Yeshua, which means "the Lord is salvation," and He lived a life that perfectly represented God in character and conduct. Therefore, to be like Him, let us be transformed by the renewing of our minds. Character and conduct begin in the mind, and our actions are affected by the things we dwell on in our thoughts. A renewed mind commits to the ideals of the Kingdom of God, and the King, who is Jesus.

Living in the world without partaking of the spirit of the world is the Christian's call. We should be setting our minds on things above and not on things on the earth. Holiness is living a life separated from the world, avoiding and rejecting the world's way of thinking. Jesus calls His people to be fully separated from the world's value system and to be totally committed to Him.

If we truly understood the fullness of our inheritance in Christ, we would not want what the world offers. When we truly come to the revelation of who Jesus is and who we are in Him, we will not want what the world offers. The believer is to gauge success by the measuring rod of God rather than by the world's social and financial standards.

Do not value worldly success. Understand that worldly assets have no spiritual or heavenly value. Hunger and thirst after the things of God and not after the perishable things this world offers. We are set apart to God and separated from the world. God cannot be glorified by those who are not fully His, neither can He be glorified by those who are of the world.

When people see us, they should be witnessing Jesus not because of us saying we are a Christian, but because the Jesus in us is shining forth. We are living in a generation where women profess Jesus Christ, but they are representing something other than Christ-like. They are displaying a lack of virtue. A lot of women do not demonstrate the ways and nature of God; they don't walk righteously. We are women that must project Christ to the world and not act like the world. We have to make choices, Godly choices, even though Godly choices involve sacrifice.

We must show ourselves to be different from the world. Satan knows if we get our eyes on the world, we are his and he is now our master. The world combined with our own carnality keeps pressuring us to conform to its attitudes and ways and it is easy for us to drift with its way of thinking. Do not love the world and all the things of the world. The desires of the old nature, the desires of the eyes, and the pretensions of life are not from our Heavenly Father but from the world. We must be women of high moral character. We must renounce the corruption that is in the world and not be part of the corruption.

What God wants is good and satisfying. God's will for us is good, acceptable, and perfect. The best way to know God's will is to be familiar with the Bible, God's Word. Virtually everything we need to know concerning the will of God is in the Bible. Once we get to know God's Word and understand it clearly, we can know the will of God. God's Word reveals to us whether we are living a soulish or spiritual life.

Once we live our lives according to God's Word, we will grow in godliness. God's Word tells us in Psalm 119:105, that His Word is a lamp to our feet and a light to our path. God's Word lights the way giving directions and wisdom for each step. We are all experiencing too much in life to be without a guide. God's Word is our guide.

Another way we can know the will of God is through prayer. Pray that His will be done in and through your life. Not your will but His will.

Pray:

> *Heavenly Father, I want Your will to be done in my life. Please guide and direct my footsteps so that I won't miss the plans and purposes that You have for my life. In Jesus name, Amen.*

Now, let's look at the definition of the word temperate:

Temperate: Self-control

We have to be women who are temperate, exercising self-control. If we lack self-control, we will be controlled by our whims. If we do not have self-control, we will be slaves to what controls us. Our appetite for pleasure can easily become our master and lead us into sin. When we have the urge to sin, we must put on self-restraint. We are to discipline our bodies and bring our bodies into submission, by abstaining from every form of evil.

When we practice self-control, we restrain ourselves from those things that are in opposition to what God is requiring. When we are tempted, self-control stops us from sinning; we pause for a while and examine our next step. When tempted by the devil, self-discipline makes us ask ourselves the right question, "Will my actions please my Heavenly Father?" Remember that He is watching, and He sees all.

Hebrews 4:13 - *And there is no creature hidden from His sight, but all things [are] naked and open to the eyes of Him to whom we [must give] account.*

So when you think that you are successful in hiding the fact that your boyfriend, male companion, or maybe that married man who is coming to you in the late hours of the night and leaving before day break, or the fact that you are living with a man in sin, and this information has been kept from your family, fellow church members, or your pastor, know that it is not kept from God. Know that we mankind (women and men) do not have a heaven or hell to put you in. But He does. And He sees all and hears all.

Romans 14:10b - *For we shall all stand before the judgment seat of Christ.*

Whether we realize it or not, we are always being watched by Him and we all shall stand before the judgment seat of Christ. Few people are conscious of the fact that He sees all, for God is omnipresent, meaning that He is present everywhere. So, what we are hiding from our neighbors, church members, family, Pastor, and friends, we are not hiding it from Him. The eyes of the Lord are in every place keeping watch on the evil and the good.

Let's all ask ourselves, if we were more conscious of God watching us, would we live a more virtuous life?

A virtuous woman consistently displays a high level of excellence in her life, practicing Godly principles that keep her growing in Godly grace. We must put to death what is earthly in ourselves: sexual immorality, impurity, passion, evil desires, in addition to developing a godly hatred for all immorality, especially sexual sin. Imitating God as His dear children.

Jesus' standards cannot be compromised and are usually in contrast to social standards of those among whom Jesus' people dwell, and His standards shun today's casual attitude toward sexual relationships. Once we have the right standards, God's standards, we can say, "No," to ourselves and then we have put on the image of God and remove the image of this world.

Morality of character is essential to the Kingdom person. God's Kingdom authority and the world's system authority are opposite to one another. We cannot let ourselves be seduced by the world's ways.

Reject the values this world has to offer you and adopt God's values. We can either choose God or satan. As Joshua says in Joshua 24:15, "Choose for yourselves this day whom you will serve."

Chapter Three
Works of the Flesh

Galatians 5:19 - *Now the works of the flesh are evident, which are: adultery, fornication, uncleanness, lewdness,*

Evidence[4]: An outward sign

Adultery[5]: Sex between a married person and someone who is not that person's wife or husband.

Fornication: Is used of illicit sexual intercourse.

Fornication[6]: Consensual sexual intercourse between two persons not married to each other.

Uncleanness: Suggestive of the fact that uncleanness is associated with sensuality.

Sensuality[7]: fleshly, gratifying bodily appetites.

---

[4] Merriam-Webster Dictionary
[5] Merriam-Webster Dictionary
[6] Merriam-Webster Dictionary
[7] Bible Dictionary

Lewdness: See the word vile.

Vile: Moral defilement.

The first works of the flesh listed in scripture can all be categorized as sexual sins. Sexual sin begins with a lustful thought, glance, or inappropriate touch. The lust of the flesh simply means wanting to gratify our body's desires at the cost of morality and what's good for our soul. The works of the flesh are the things we naturally tend towards that are contrary to God's design for us. Temptations to gratify our sexual desires are flung at us all the time.

Fornication is not just tolerated in our society but is actually being encouraged. When we turn on the TV, we are exposed to allurements to fornication, adultery, and many other sexual acts. Through what is on TV, there are desires created by the programming and the commercials to allure us to follow the cravings of our flesh. TV shows promote fornicating with every man we meet and/or just met, orgies, committing adultery, wife swapping, men having multiple wives, and they are all co-habiting together. They even portray Christians and Pastors fornicating, committing adultery, wife swapping, having multiple wives co-habiting together, etc. It is sad to say that a lot of this is going on in some churches. It is there every day, all day long, for you to see.

These TV shows promote that this is good behavior, that this is okay to do, and that this is the norm for today's society. Today's society is preoccupied with sex, sexual desires, and lust. These temptations influence our conduct and many women have fallen into this type of lifestyle because of wanting to gratify their body's desires. They have been influenced and are constantly being influenced by the world's values.

We should not allow our sexual desires to determine our lifestyle. People who are controlled by the lust of the flesh have no respect for the lifestyle of the godly. Such people delight in enticing others into sin. Thinking and doing as the world thinks and does will unavoidably lead to sensuality and impurity, and when our sexual desires are given free rein, we live as if we do not bear God's image. We cannot hold onto this world with one hand and hold onto our Lord and Savior with the other.

Evidence

What are you evidencing in your life? Are you evidencing the works of the flesh, adultery, fornication, uncleanness, or lewdness?

Are you proclaiming to be a Christian, a believer, daughter of the Most High, but at the same time gratifying your body's desires at the cost of morality and what's good for your soul?

What are you exhibiting to the world? Are you Christ-like or world-like?

Your actions and your lifestyle demonstrate the choices you have made, not what you say out of your mouth. Your actions speak much, much louder than words.

Fornication and Adultery

The word "fornication" includes all acts of immorality, which is sin. It includes premarital sex, pornography, illicit sexual intercourse, prostitution, whoredom, incest, licentiousness, and adultery. Galatians 5:19, the scripture at the beginning of this chapter, is saying that we should not be involved in any sexual immorality, impurity, indecency, orgies, and things like this. There is sexual immorality among many Christian women, and there should not be any sexual immorality or any kind of impurity. This is inappropriate for God's people because these have no share in the kingdom.

Do you not know that the unrighteous will not inherit the kingdom of God?

*1 **Corinthians** 7:1-2 ESV - Now concerning the matters about which you wrote: "It is good for a man not to have sexual relations with a woman."*
7:2 - But because of the temptation to sexual immorality, each man should have his own wife and each woman her own husband.

In the above scriptures, Apostle Paul was addressing a question that was written to him, "Is it good for a man to abstain from sex with women?" Paul's response was that because of the danger of sexual immorality, each man should have his own wife and each woman her own husband.

In order to guard against sexual immorality, God has ordained the sacred relationship of marriage. Leaving our parents home, cleaving to our spouse, and living together as two who have become one is for marriage only. Marriage is the one and only place that God has provided for sexual union to take place. Marriage is honorable in every respect and sex within marriage is pure. Outside of marriage it is destructive and a clear defiance of God's design.

Sexual intercourse is an intimate expression of affection between a husband and wife. The Bible calls it a privilege and a mystery by which two people, a man and a woman, become one flesh. The privilege is abused when people not married to each other have intercourse, then that which God meant for blessing becomes a cause of judgment.

Ephesians 5:31 - *"For this reason a man shall leave his father and mother and be joined to his wife, and the two shall become one flesh."*
5:32 - This is a great mystery, but I speak concerning Christ and the church.

Many people who say they are Christians and profess Christ as their Savior are living in sin with someone and acting like they are married, and are justifying their lifestyle by saying:

1. "We are living together for financial reasons."
2. "We are living together to see if we are compatible."
3. "We are planning on getting married."

There is premarital sex in the world, but in the Bible, in the eyes of God, premarital sex is not His design. Paul wrote to the early church, admonishing them to abstain from fornication. Those instructions were good for the early church, and it remains good instruction for us today.

Acts 15:20 - *"but that we write to them to abstain from things polluted by idols, [from] sexual* *immorality, [from] things strangled, and [from] blood.*

Another Bible translation reads:

Instead, we should write them a letter telling them to abstain from things polluted by idols, from fornication, from what is strangled and from blood.

The Church must sustain a Biblical commitment to sexual purity and moral self-control. We are to abstain from all acts of fornication, not to contemplate evil passions and desires in our thought life, not thinking or acting on strong sexual desires. Our self-produced desires should not be satisfied but be controlled, that each of us know how to manage our sexual impulses in a holy and honorable manner. If you are not able to control your flesh, then your flesh will control you.

Hebrews 13:4 - *Marriage [is] honorable among all, and the bed undefiled; but fornicators and adulterers God will judge.*

The above scripture is saying marriage is honorable in every respect and in particular, sex within marriage is pure but God will indeed punish fornicators and adulterers. Adultery goes against

God's Word, it defiles the marriage covenant made before God, and it destroys the family structure. It is incompatible with the harmonious laws of family life in God's Kingdom, and it violates God's original purpose in marriage. God rejects adultery and will always judge it severely.

The Ten Commandments contain the prohibition against adultery; "You shall not commit adultery." Whoever commits adultery lacks sense, whoever does it destroys themselves. Adultery causes damage. It is very hurtful to the spouse and most times it leads to divorce and bitterness. Children are very damaged because the security of a healthy home is broken, and it denies them a role model for a healthy, loving marriage. Flee from and detest adultery and honor marriage fidelity.

Uncleanness and Lewdness

Uncleanness and lewdness begin in the mind as unclean thoughts, and these thoughts eventually produce lewd and/or unclean actions. When the Bible speaks of uncleanness and lewdness, it refers to the absence of spiritual purity and holiness. There are many women who live the lifestyle of lewdness and uncleanness, living a life of defilement, living a life of unashamed indecency, unbridled lust, unrestrained depravity, and unnatural lust. When we purposely live without restraints, we are living in the darkened lifestyle of lewdness, doing something that we know is wrong but doing it anyway because it feels good, indulging in excess sexual behavior in many different areas of our life.

Are we going to listen to God or do what satisfies our flesh? We must choose who will be our master – the lust of the flesh or the Spirit of God. Let us not set our affections on or live sacrificially on behalf of anything that appeals to our fleshly appetites. Flee from sexual immorality, for this is the will of God, that we abstain from sexual immorality and that we know how to control our own body in holiness and honor. Flee passions and pursue righteousness.

The Word tells us:

Ephesians 5:1 - *Therefore be imitators of God as dear children.*

The key phrase in this scripture is:
   1.   Be imitators of God.

Godly behavior is modeling ourselves after Him and imitating Him rather than imitating the world. He is our perfect example. Understand that imitating God as dear children will keep us from moral corruption. Godliness is living the way He wants us to live, because He gave His only begotten Son on our behalf in order to free us from all sin and purify for Himself a people who would be His own and eager to do good. Do not be deceived, we should not be led by our flesh or our sexual desires.

By the evidence we are exhibiting, being led by our flesh and sexual desires, we are denying Him. We should be led by the Spirit and not be led by our flesh.

The Bible tells us that Sodom, Gomorrah, and the surrounding cities gave themselves over to sexual immorality and went after strange flesh. Therefore, God judged Sodom, Gomorrah, and the surrounding cities by raining down fire and sulfur upon them until they were totally destroyed. Now, these cities serve as an example to us of suffering the vengeance of eternal fire in hell, which is what awaits the immoral.

CHAPTER FOUR
Modesty

Modesty[8]: The quality, in women, of dressing or behaving in a way that is intended to avoid attracting sexual interest.

In the past, modesty was considered to be a very important virtue. Modesty is the outward expression of purity of thoughts and manners, with due regard for propriety in speech and actions; it also includes chastity and self-control. A modestly dressed woman speaks and acts in a manner that support and encourage purity and chastity. She does not act in a manner that would tempt or encourage sinful sexual behavior.

Women are to be modest in their appearance and not display all the attractions of her body or a hint of sexual provocativeness. Women should wear decent and appropriate clothing and not draw attention to themselves and to their private body parts. Women dressing this way are only degrading themselves. Lack of modesty includes dressing in a way to

---

[8] Cambridge English Dictionary

visually stimulate men in order to provoke them to sexual lust, by emphasizing private parts of the body, like wearing tight and revealing clothing.

Provocative: To stir what is evil in another.

Provocative[9]: Serving or tending to provoke, excite, stimulate.

Provocative[10]: Exciting sexual desire.

All definitions define the word provocative to provoke, to stir, stimulate, and excite sexual desires. Dressing and/or acting provocatively has a very specific purpose, to shock, titillate, and stimulate. Stimulation is mostly the reason for minimal and skin-tight fashion that we see today. It is saying, "look how sexy I am." A woman who intentionally dresses in a provocative way is a temptress, because dressing provocatively produces temptation, tempting men to lust after our body.

Matthew 5:28 - *But I say to you that whoever looks at a woman to lust for her has already committed adultery with her in his heart.*

Sexual sin begins with a glance and lustful thought(s), so when someone dresses provocatively

---

[9] Merriam Webster Dictionary

[10] Vocabulary.com

they are causing men to sin by lusting after their body. Some women might not realize how their dressing affects men; they are just wearing what they think looks good.

A Japanese friend of mine recently told me that when she was younger and got her first office job, she wore sexy clothes. She only did this because she thought it was fashionable; she was not trying to entice anyone. She said that she wished someone had taken her aside and showed her how to dress. She had no idea that the kind of apparel she was wearing was inappropriate and distracting. She said, "I just didn't know, no one told me or showed me the correct way." So now being older and wiser, whenever she sees a young woman in her surroundings and if she has a chance to speak to her, she will speak up.

Recently she had a chance to speak to someone in her neighborhood who was dressed very provocatively. By talking to the young woman, she found out she was on her way to a meeting, she came right out and asked her, "What kind of service are you selling dressed like that?" She began to speak to her about her provocative dressing and told her that no woman would want her around her husband dressed like that and she should be more modest in her dressing. My friend mentioned again that she wished someone would have told her, so now her mission is to tell other women.

I was talking to another woman who I have had a couple of conversations with. I was telling her about a product that I purchased at a store. She told me that she has one of the same stores near her, but she refuses to go there because when she goes there, all she sees is women with their breasts hanging out. Now this woman has not yet given her life to the Lord, but even the unsaved can recognize the inappropriate, provocative, and immoral ways women are dressing.

But many women *do* realize how effective their provocative dressing is and they know exactly what they are doing. What we wear sends a message whether we intend to or not. If we are flaunting our bodies, men will be tempted and come after our body because that is what is being advertised. Female private body parts do entice males, sexually tempting them, and a lot of men do give into that temptation to commit fornication and adultery.

Women, when you dress provocatively and advertise your body parts, men may want to, and will, spend a night with you, but they do not want to spend their life with you. No godly man will ever go for an indecent woman for marriage. If you dress provocatively, a godly man will always behold nothing good in you, and an ungodly man will only see you as a sex toy for satisfying his sexual desires.

I grew up with two parents in the home and I was the only daughter. I was a daddy's girl and always wanted to be with my dad. He gave me much love and attention and showed me that I was special to him. A father is the first relationship that a daughter has with a man; he teaches and shows his daughter how a woman should be treated by a man.

Unfortunately, there are many women who did not have a dad growing up. They did not have a dad to give them love and attention to give them the validation which they are seeking and hungry for. A dad who is in his daughter's life will validate his daughter through love and attention and teach her self-worth. When there is no daddy around to hug, love, and encourage the daughter, there is an emptiness inside of her – a void. Many women are sleeping with different men to fill this void and emptiness, because they are hungry for love and attention. They are seeking worthiness, approval, and acceptance; they want to feel and know that they have value and worth. This is what is lacking in many women's lives because they did not receive it as a little girl while they were growing up.

Many women are dressing for attention, they feel starved for male attention, and believe that any attention is good attention. It is a tragedy that women of all ages struggle with this issue, struggling with the desires to be wanted. We as women tend to offer too much of ourselves to men for that attention, but the only attention we are getting is sexual attention.

Women know men want sex and men know women want love. So women, including women who say they are Christian, use sex to get love. But it is not love that we are getting; it is only sex. And men will claim to love us just to get the sex.

Many reality TV shows demonstrate women in competition with other women trying to win the prize, the guy. They (not all but the majority) dress very provocatively, revealing way too much of their bodies, so they can have a better chance in getting the guy or a date with the guy. It is sad that so many women feel that they have to use their sexuality to get what they want. Many women have conformed to this world, and they have bought into the worldly desires and the world's way of thinking.

In nations where there are kings and queens ruling, does the queen (wife of a king) or a female leader of a nation, or a princess (daughter of a king) go around dressing provocatively, half dressed, showing the private parts of their body, and wearing tight fitting clothes? The answer is **no**.

Why? Because:

1. They are representing their nation.
2. They are representing royalty, the kingdom, the throne.
3. They are representing the royal family and the family name.
4. They have self-respect because they were taught self-respect.

The late Princes Diana of the British Royal family, daughter-in-law to late Queen Elizabeth II of the United Kingdom, represented her position as Princess of Wales with style and grace. She was and still is considered as one of the most fashionable and stylish females of her time. She dressed with modesty and even though she dressed modestly she was considered a fashionable, classy, stylish, and elegant woman. She was showcased in a lot of magazines because of her stylish dressing.

Jackie Kennedy, First Lady of the United States, the late wife of the late President John Kennedy, was also one who dressed modestly and was considered fashionable, stylish, and elegant. She too was showcased in many magazines because of her stylish dressing. She represented the United States as well as the Kennedy name. Melania Trump, another First Lady of the United States, wife of former President Donald Trump, also dresses modestly but she dresses with style, grace, and she is very fashionable in her way of dressing.

Female Ambassadors at the United Nations representing their country/nation do not dress provocatively, wearing tight fitting clothes, revealing clothes exposing their private body parts; they dress modestly.

Ambassadors at the United Nations are representatives of their nations. They are sent to act on their nation's behalf not to speak for their own self-interest, not acting in their own will, but the good will for their nation. Some of them, when they address the United Nations, speak in their nation's language. As ambassadors for Christ should we not also be speaking words that represent His Kingdom and not words that represent the social standards of this world which is passing away and the lust of it?

2 Corinthians 5:20 - *Now then, we are ambassadors for Christ, as though God were pleading through us: we implore [you] on Christ's behalf, be reconciled to God.*

This means that as born-again Christians, we are royalty in the Kingdom of Heaven.

Philippians 3:20 - *For our citizenship is in heaven, from which we also eagerly wait for the Savior, the Lord Jesus Christ,*

This is saying that our citizenship and ultimate residence is in heaven. We are ambassadors for Christ and here on earth we are representing our King and Savior. We want to show people around us that we are not from here, we want them to see that we are different. Different by our actions, words, and deeds. We want to be that shining bright light in this very dark world.

As ambassadors of Christ, we should be speaking heavenly language not sexual innuendoes.

Romans 8:15 - *For you did not receive the spirit of bondage again to fear, but you received the Spirit of adoption by whom we cry out, "Abba, Father."*

8:16 - The Spirit Himself bears witness with our spirit that we are children of God,

8:17 - and if children, then heirs--heirs of God and joint heirs with Christ, if indeed we suffer with [Him], that we may also be glorified together.

This means that when we were saved, we became adopted sons and daughters of God. We are adopted into God's royal family. God calls us His children and we became heirs of God and joint-heirs with

Jesus Christ.

Understand and know that we are representing Jesus Christ, we are representing God's Kingdom, we are representing the Throne, and we are representing the Royal Family. Understand that He has a standard that is required of us, and we should be dressing, acting, and speaking in accordance with His standards.

There are many women who attend church wearing provocative attire. They sit on the front pew of the church with tight dresses up to their thighs and when they sit down or bend over, people have a full view of their under clothes. Or, they wear a very low cut top so that it looks like their breasts might fall out. A lot of churches are not addressing these issues. They are allowing women to come into the House of the Lord dressed this way and it is not a representation of Christ. Do you think Abba Father is pleased with this going on in the house of God? No, He is not.

Many women do not have self-respect because they were not taught this at home. Many women complain that they aren't treated with respect but look at the way they are dressing and carrying themselves, they dress provocatively, act provocatively, behave seductively, and expect to be treated with respect. They can't have it both ways. They will be treated exactly how they present themselves, and they will not get respect if they don't respect themselves.

I heard two men talking and the subject was how women are dressing these days. One of them said that it is fun to look at but hard to respect. Another time, I was talking to a nineteen-year-old male who was in his second year of college. He shared that he feels that the young women today feel that the only way they can get a man's attention is to show their body off by dressing provocatively. He also thinks that they do not have any morals and values of a proper woman. Even at this young man's age, he has observed the same thing about how women are dressing. Women, we need to realize our responsibility to dress modestly and to behave in a way that is not seductive.

Society has changed the role that was traditionally for men and boys. The roles have been reversed and women are the ones left in charge of romantic pursuits and brazenly chasing men. Men do not have to approach women because women are doing the approaching now.

I was talking to another young man who was eighteen years old and in his first year of college. I was telling him not to be focused on looking at the girls. He gave me a smile and a certain look and said, "They are looking at me." What he was saying was he did not have to focus on them or approach them because they were approaching and pursuing him. Women are not letting men be men; they are now taking on the role of the man by being the pursuer.

I was watching a TV show and a man relocated halfway across the United States to a small town. He had only been in the new town for about two days and this woman approached him. During their conversation, she told him there were not many men around their age in the town. From my observation, they were both in their mid-thirties. She told the guy that she has dated many men in the town, and most were on drugs or had been in prison. She said she wanted to be the first woman to approach him before the other women started noticing him around town. Then, she asked to buy him dinner. Here's how their conversation went:

"Can I buy you dinner?"
"No, I can't let you do that."
"Why? Are you married? You got a girlfriend?"
"No."
"Come on, let me buy you dinner."
"No, I can't let you do that."

Saddened, she turned to walk away and as she was leaving, he said to her, "But *I* can buy *you* dinner!"

The look on her face was one of surprise. He refused to let her take the role of the man. He had been taught how to treat a woman. And in his training, he was taught that the man asks the woman out and pays for the meal. As a man, he could not let her pay for the meal. He told her twice, "I can't let you do that," but she was not hearing what he was saying. Women are missing out on how to be treated like a lady by a man because they are not letting the men be gentlemen.

One day on my way to church, I stopped at a store to get a cup of coffee. As I was approaching the door a man, who was not at the door, said from a distance, "Let me get the door for you," and he started jogging to the door so I would not have to wait long for him. I said to him, "I will not deny you from being a gentleman." He opened the door for me, and I thanked him and told him to have a good day. I went in one direction to get my coffee and he went in another direction.

While I was fixing my coffee, he came over to get his coffee and he said, "I am going to pay for your coffee." At first, I thought he was joking, so I said, "okay," and continued to fix my coffee. By the time I had finished fixing my coffee, I sensed in my spirit that he was not joking. So I said to him, "I will be waiting up front at the cash register for you." And he said, "I will tell the cashier that I am going to pay for

41

your coffee." He walked up front and told the cashier that he was paying for my coffee, and to put it on his bill. I thanked him and walked out of the store.

When I got in my vehicle, I immediately thanked the Lord for blessing me with a free cup of coffee, I thanked the Lord for putting it in the man's heart to bless me with a cup of coffee, and I thanked the Lord for starting my day off with a good blessing.

When I got to church, I told two Christian women at separate times how the Lord started my day off with the blessing of a free cup of coffee. Both women at separate times, asked me the very same question, "Did you get his phone number?" I told each of them that I did not. They wanted to know why not, and I said the same thing to both women, "If that is who God had for me, then I would not have to ask him for his phone number." One of women said to me, "Sometimes men need help," and I said to her, "If this is who God had for me or if this was a divine connection then conversation would have taken place and contact information would have been exchanged."

Understand that God does not need our help. God does not need our help by having us (women) ask a man for his phone number or pursue him. We need God's help. God is more than able to put it in a man's heart to ask you for your phone number if that is who He has for you or if it's a divine connection.

Jeremiah 32:27 *- Behold, I [am] the LORD, the God of all flesh. Is there anything too hard for Me?*

Luke 1:37 *- For with God nothing will be impossible.*

He is the God of every living creature. God is omnipotent, meaning all powerful. He created the universe, heavens, and the earth. He created you. And do you really think God needs your help in doing anything? That He needs your help by having you pursue men?

Proverbs 18:22 *- [He who] finds a wife finds a good [thing], And obtains favor from the LORD.*

We do not have to pursue a man. Just because a man speaks to us or even behaves in a gentlemanly way, does not mean it is an invitation to pursue him or that he wants to be pursued. The man opening the door for me and buying me a cup of coffee is not a reason for me to offer my phone number to him or ask for his phone number. I was very surprised that *both* Christian women asked the same question, and *both* of their comments and mindsets were on pursuing the man. So, this is an example that even some Christian women's minds are also on pursuing men, meaning the world's way of doing things.

I want to be treated like a lady and I expect to be treated like a lady because I am a lady. I expect a man to open the door for me. When I go to a store, if a man is at the door and opens the door for me, even young men and boys, I always thank them and say to them, "thank you sir," because I want them to know that I appreciate and acknowledge their gentlemanly act. Especially the young men and boys - I want to give them acknowledgement, appreciation, and to encourage them so they can keep on acting like a gentleman. When riding in the car with a man, I do not open my car door when I am getting in or getting out. That is the role of the man being a gentleman. I expect a man to help me with my coat. Women, in order to be treated like a lady, you have to carry yourself like a lady which means your speech, your dress and your actions should reflect that of a lady. Let men be men. Stop taking on the role of a man. When you take on the role of the man, you are missing out on how it feels to be treated like a lady. Dressing provocatively will not get you the lady treatment, but it will get you the sex object treatment.

Many women have low self-esteem, they feel worthless, they feel they have no value, they feel they have no one to love them, and/or no one has ever loved them. Because of this, they will allow themselves to be treated any kind of way by a man because they are afraid of losing him. Having him is better than not having him because they do not want to be alone.

Many women feel that they are not complete unless they have a man in their life. But God's Word says in Colossians 2:10 that we are complete in Him. In your union with Christ, you have been made complete and full. It's in this union with Christ that the old nature's control over your body was stripped away. Thinking that you are not complete without a man means that you are only pandering to the flesh and not edifying yourself in the truth. The truth is that we are complete in Christ and not in a man. In order to be complete in Christ we have to give our lives to Christ. We need to have a relationship with Him. It's not about religion, it's about a relationship.

You have a Father, a Heavenly Father. He has always been there for you, you just didn't know it; or maybe you did know it but just did not acknowledge Him; or maybe you pushed Him to the side. Some of you have a broken spirit because of life's difficulties. He knows of your pain, hurt, disappointments, and your rejections - He knows it all. He has always been there waiting for you to cry out to Him, to call to Him, to come to Him, and He has always been there waiting for you with open arms to love you, to comfort you, to protect you, to give you peace, provide for you, heal your hurt, pain, to pick up the shattered pieces of your heart and put it back together, to bring wholeness to you (nothing missing nothing broken) and to deliver you. He has always been there. You may not have received validation from your earthly father, but your Heavenly Father, who loves you, has already validated you. God approved you because He created you. You are His creation you were made in His image.

Genesis 1:26—*Then God said Let us make humankind in Our image in the likeness of Ourselves; and let them rule over the fish in the sea, the birds in the air, the animals, and over all the earth, and over every crawling creature that crawls on the earth.*
1:27—*So God created humankind in His own Image; in the image of God He created him: male and female He created them.*[11]

The above scripture proves our validation. There is no higher validation than God's validation. We were made in His image according to His likeness. There is no one, and there is nothing higher than the One true living God, our Heavenly Father, Yahweh, our Creator, the God of Abraham, Isaac, and Jacob. Just think about it. We were made in His image according

---

[11] The Complete Jewish Study Bible

to His likeness. There is no one and there is nothing more powerful than Yahweh. He is Omnipotent and He gave us the choice to walk in power and authority.

Acts 1:8 - *But you shall receive power when the Holy Spirit has come upon you; and you shall be witnesses to Me in Jerusalem, and in all Judea and Samaria, and to the end of the earth.*

John 14:12 - *Most assuredly, I say to you, he who believes in Me, the works that I do he will do also; and greater [works] than these he will do,*

There is no greater love than His love.

Romans 5:8 - *But God demonstrates His own love toward us, in that while we were still sinners, Christ died for us.*

This means that we did not have to make ourselves righteous before God decided to send Jesus Christ to earn our salvation. God demonstrated His own love for us in that Jesus Christ died on our behalf while we were still sinners. That while we were rebellious, undeserving, and ungodly people, God poured out His love in Jesus Christ.

John 3:16 - *For God so loved the world that He gave His only begotten Son, that whoever believes in*

Him should not perish but have everlasting life.

God does not make mistakes. You are a beautiful creation from God.

Psalm 139:13 - *For You formed my inward parts; You covered me in my mother's womb.*
139:14 - *I will praise You, for I am fearfully [and] wonderfully made; Marvelous are Your works, And [that] my soul knows very well.*

Understand and know that you have already been validated, you have value, you have worth, and you have a purpose. The only approval we should be seeking is God's approval not man's approval. See yourself the way Jesus sees you. He chose you to be here for such a time as this.

So, ladies, we can dress modestly and still be fashionable and be stylish and dress with class. There is a difference between being attractive and attracting. How we dress, what we speak, and how we treat people reflects how we feel on the inside. If we advertise who we are on the inside, having morals, integrity, values, self-respect, having self-control, speaking good things, being kind, having joy, and living a holy life unto the Lord, then we will get the respect and the sons of God will be drawn to us. We humans focus on the outward appearance, but not

God. The scripture is very clear that it's what's on the inside that matters to God. The heart is what matters.

1 Samuel 16:7 - But the LORD said to Samuel, "Do not look at his appearance or at his physical stature, because I have refused him. For [the LORD does] not [see] as man sees; for man looks at the outward appearance, but the LORD looks at the heart."

Many women are not representing Christ and our Father's Heavenly Kingdom here on earth - they are representing satan's kingdom. Know that Satan's kingdom enslaves its citizens with darkened hearts and minds and women are blindly following their master and leader. The one who they are bowing down to, satan, is pulling them deeper into sin so that they can remain captives in his kingdom of sin headed for destruction. They are walking according to the course of this world, satan's world, where half dressed women are glorified. They are fulfilling the lust of their flesh and of the mind. Their body will not get them what they want, but the favor of the Lord will. Aggressively pursue Jesus and not a man.

CHAPTER FIVE

Your Children

Psalm 127:3 - *Behold, children [are] a heritage from the LORD, The fruit of the womb [is] a reward.*

The Complete Jewish Study Bible reads:

Psalm 127:3 - *Children are a gift from Adonai the fruit of the womb is a reward.*

At age eighteen, I became pregnant within my first year of college. I did not tell my parents that I was pregnant because I did not want them to be ashamed and disappointed in me for my actions. I told a relative of mine who lived in Washington, D.C. that I was pregnant, and they suggested that I come there to get an abortion. Shortly thereafter, I told the father of my child that I was pregnant, and then I left college and headed to Washington, D.C. to get an abortion. When I spoke to the child's father, I did not mention that I was in Washington, D.C. to get an abortion.

Up until this point, an abortion never entered my

mind. It was not something that I thought of or would have thought of. I did not want my parents to be ashamed and disappointed in me for my actions, so I did not tell them either.

At the clinic in Washington, D.C., they told me I would need to apply for Medicaid to get an abortion. I had no idea what Medicaid was. All I knew was that I needed Medicaid to get the abortion. They told me where I needed to go to apply for a Medicaid card and another relative drove me there.

When we got to the building, the line was very long and extended outside at the end of the building. It was a very cold day, and the line was moving very slowly. It took hours before I reached the door of the building. When I finally got to the desk, the woman asked me what I was there for, and I said Medicare.

Now at that time I did not know what Medicare was, but that is what came out of my mouth. Understand that I was born and raised in a very small southern country town. I had never heard of Medicaid or Medicare. I did not know any adults that had health issues. I had never heard anyone say Mr. or Mrs. so-and-so is sick, so I had never heard of Medicaid or Medicare. I had never heard my parents mention either word. Everyone I knew who became pregnant gave birth and had their child. I had never heard anyone talk about abortion or heard of anyone having one, so I was ignorant about those things.

One thing I was not ignorant about was not to have sex before marriage. I was taught at home and at church that sex before marriage is a sin, it goes against God's Word, and the consequences of your sinful actions could end up in pregnancy. I did get pregnant the very first and only time I had sex. So yes, you can get pregnant the first time you have sex - I am an example of that. Some people might say that it was just bad luck or that I was just unlucky, but I do not believe in luck or something being a coincidence.

So, I stood in the cold in that line for many hours to get my one chance and I said the wrong word, "Medicare." The woman immediately said to me, "You are too young for Medicare. Next in line." Then, she immediately turned to the next girl in line and started addressing her.

I walked away thinking I said the wrong word. I had not heard of the word Medicaid and I did not know what it was, other than this is what I need to get an abortion. I had practiced saying the word over and over on my way to the place so I would not get it wrong. And I got it wrong.

I walked out of the building and saw that the line was still long, so I said I would come back tomorrow and ask for the right thing. All I could think about is that if she knew I was too young for Medicare, why did she not help me out and say you mean Medicaid?

But God had other plans which I did not know then, but I know now. Once I got back to where I was staying in Washington, D.C., my relative asked me what happened. I told her I asked for Medicare instead of Medicaid and I would go back the next day.

But after that conversation, abortion never entered my mind again. I never thought about getting an abortion and I never again mentioned the word abortion. Abortion was completely wiped from my mind. The relative who gave me a ride told me that they would come back the next day and take me back, but they never called me to ask what time I wanted to be picked up. The relative who suggested that I come to Washington D.C. never asked me when I was going back to apply for Medicaid so I could get the abortion, and they never mentioned the word abortion again. It was like God had wiped abortion from all our minds. The only thing I would think about is that I must prepare for this baby. And that is what I did.

When I was a few months pregnant, I moved to

Maryland. After I had the baby, I contacted the father of my child and told him the sex of the child, his name, gave him my phone number, and told him if he wished to see his child to let me know. He never called and I never called him again. I did not have time to focus on him because I had to focus on my child and other issues.

When my child was about nine months old, I moved back to Washington, D.C. for a few weeks, then I moved back to my home state of Virginia (but not back home with my parents) for three years, and then I moved back to Maryland for about a year. It was a lot of moving. But when my son was going to start Kindergarten, I moved to a different part of Maryland, and we stayed there until he graduated from high school.

I put my life on hold because it was no longer about me; it was all about this precious child of mine. I had to take care of and protect my son. I was always conscious about keeping a good image as a mother in front of my child. How I lived my life in front of my son was very important to me.

The only men I would allow to come inside my home were relatives and men I grew up with or went to school with. I did not let men inside my home because in the back of my mind I would be thinking,

"What if he turned out to be someone who would molest my son?" The only time my son saw me with a man is when I was in a long-term relationship and in that relationship the three of us did things together. My son was never left out, even when we went out of town, my son went with us. I did not want my son to see me dating different men. To me that was not a good image for a son to see. I did not have drinking in my home. I did not drink, so I did not allow any alcohol in my home and any drinking around my son. I did not use profanity, so you could not use profanity in my home or around my son.

When my son was very young, I asked him if he wanted to know about his father and he told me "No." In his teen years he did ask me about his father, and I told him what I knew but that I did not know where he was. Not once have I ever talked negatively about my son's father to my son or anyone else. I never put him down and I never said anything bad about him. I told my son we had been young, and that I did not know what was going through his mind or what had happened in his life before I met him. After I got pregnant, I did not know what frame of mind he was in or what he was dealing with at that time. I told my son that if he ever met him, then he could find out the answers to his questions. This is honestly how I felt. I never spoke anything bad about him and I never will.

My mother was a strong woman of faith and a praying woman. She mentioned to me about a year or two after my son had graduated from high school, that she had been praying to the Lord for my son to meet his father. I don't know how long she had been praying this prayer. I was surprised that I never thought to pray about it, so I prayed that they would meet and that his father would accept him.

After my son got married my daughter-in-law was the one to encourage my son in seeking out his dad to find out who he is. She mentioned to me that she had been searching online for any information, but she was not having any success. She asked me if I could help in locating his dad.

I started searching online for information, but I came up with zero information. Then one day it came to me, I don't know where he is, but I know who does. I know that the Lord knows because He knows all things. So, I prayed to the Lord to reveal to me where he was, to let him and my son meet, and let him accept my son and not reject him. Every time I would go to Calvary Pentecostal Tabernacle (CPT), I would take a certain route which took me past the parent's home of someone I went to college with who had married my son's father's cousin. There were several routes I could have taken but I always took this route.

In April 2014, about six months after my prayer to the Lord to reveal the location of my son's dad, the Lord answered my prayers. One weekend when I was at CPT, I had just gotten out of service when the Holy Spirit said to me, "Tomorrow, don't forget to stop by the house." I immediately knew what the Holy Spirit was saying to me. The Holy Spirit was telling me to stop by the parent's house of the girl who attended the same college I did, who I wanted to get information from about my son's dad.

The next day after service, I went to her parent's home. Her mother answered the door and I introduced myself and told her who my dad was – everyone knew my dad. I told her I attended college with her daughter, and I wanted to know how I could get in contact with her. She told me that her daughter lives in Georgia and that she just arrived from Georgia because she also has a home right down the road from her. She told me that she had just left, so I could catch her at her home, and she gave me directions for how to get there. I knew that this was nobody but God at work; this was a divine connection. God put this together.

I did as her mother instructed me and went to visit her. She told me that she and a few college mates had been talking about me a few weeks ago, wondering what had happened to me. I felt bad because I could not put a face to the names of the people that were asking about me. She told me that she just came in from Georgia and that she came back home to attend a week of services that were going on at her home church. I told her I had gotten pregnant by my son's dad, and I was trying to locate him because my son wanted to meet him. She informed me that she and her husband had not stayed in contact with my son's dad and that he had died a couple years ago. I was very saddened to hear this and asked her for the details about his passing. She told me she had his brother's number, and she called his brother to find out if she could give me the number and if he would talk to me. He agreed. I called him and introduced myself and what he said to me surprised me. He told me he knew about my son. His brother had told him that he had a son. In fact, he told everyone that he had a son. But everyone thought that he was lying because he was always strung out on drugs, so everyone thought it was the drugs talking. He apologized for not getting in contact with my son. He said his brother had died and I told him I could not go back and tell that to my son – that I have to take him something back other than death. I asked him if he had any other children and he told me about his daughter and he gave me her number so my son could call her. He also said my son could call him if he wanted to talk.

I called my son and told him the news. I told him that his uncle said he could call him, and he would talk to him, and that he has a sister, and I gave him both numbers. I told my son that God did not allow him to meet his dad for a reason because God was more than able to make it happen and He did not. And because He did not make it happen, He must not want it to happen, so I believe that God was protecting him from something and maybe we would never know, but I know there is a reason why He did not allow it to happen.

My son called me the next day telling me that he called his sister, and he told her who he was, but she was not responding much so he hung up thinking he would give her time to digest the news. But the next day she called him on his job and told him she thought that he was someone who was trying to get money from her but after they had hung up, she googled him online and saw his picture and all she could see was her dad and knew that this was him. She also told him that their dad told her when she was just a little girl that she had a brother, and that he would tell everyone he has a son, but no one believed him. She even told him at one point their father was looking for him in Virginia because that is where he thought he was.

I was told by my son that they talked a few hours,

and she told him that their father was a heroin addict. After leaving college (I do not know if he graduated or left early) his life was a struggle with drugs. It was only two years before he died that he got clean from drugs. His early death was the result of him being on drugs the majority of his life. In the course of their conversation, my son told her that he was into making films and he and his friend had co-produced some films together, that he had taken some courses in filming, and loves documentaries. She told him that if he knew her life's story about being on drugs, he might want to do a film. Near the end of their conversation, she wanted them to meet in person and she invited him to come meet her. I am not sure how long after this conversation this took place, but I know it was not long.

My son and his wife went to meet his sister. On Saturday they met at a restaurant (I believe it was a restaurant) and then they spent that day together. The following day they went to her home for dinner and when he arrived, he was surprised to discover that his sister had invited all his relatives to come to meet him. He met his family for the very first time; he got to meet all his aunts and his uncle, nephew, niece, and cousins. Everyone embraced him, especially the aunts because they said he looked just like their brother. Their brother, my son's father, was the youngest of the siblings and his sisters spoiled him. I was told that his aunts became emotional when they saw him. My daughter-in-law was filming the entire event and they showed me the film when they got back. I heard my son say to everyone, "I want you to know that my mother never said anything bad about my dad, she never said anything negative about him I just want you to know this."

My son told me that after hearing that his dad and sister were strung out on drugs, he believed that God did protect him. He said he very well could have gotten pulled into that lifestyle with them by wanting to be accepted by them. Alternatively, if he had met them while they were on drugs, he would have judged them by saying they are nothing but drug addicts. He would never want to be bothered with them again.

My son and his sister have a great relationship and they visit each other often – even his sister's mom accepts him. My daughter-in-law told me that on one visit to see his sister and aunts they walked into his sister's home and her mom was on the phone and told the person on the phone, "I have to go my son just walked in." Just last summer (2021) his sister's sister (which is not my son's sister) came up to the National Harbor and she called my son and told him she was here, so he and his wife went to see her. She brought a male friend with her and introduced him to my son and told my son, he (her boyfriend) is trying to be your brother-in-law. Even she thinks of him as her brother. Look at God.

I prayed to the Lord to let his dad accept him and not reject him, but God went beyond what I prayed for. He gave my son favor and acceptance from the entire family. The first time his sister came to visit, he brought her over to meet me. I have been told several times by my son and daughter-in-law that the family, especially the aunts, ask when I am coming to meet them.

My son did hear his sister's story on being a drug addict and he did a documentary on her drug addiction struggles. She started off in high school drinking and said one reason for going down this destructive road was she wanted more attention from her dad and wanted to spend more time with him. She went from drinking to marijuana to cocaine to crack and was a crack addict.

If you want to see the documentary that my son produced on his sister, it is called Divine Intervention Savage to Sobriety located at: https://www.youtube.com/watch?v=U2yhozXaTkg.

When my son and his sister met, she was off drugs, she had given her life to the Lord and had received

Jesus as her Lord and Savior. Because she has given her life to Jesus, her life has changed. She has gone back to school, attained her degree, opened up a health center to counsel drug addicts, and she is also a Pastor. See, God did not allow my son to meet his dad or his sister while they were still strung out on drugs. It was only after his sister was saved that He allowed the meeting to take place. My mother died in January 2014, four months before my son was united with his family, so she never got to see the manifestation of what she prayed for.

My testimony is that God stepped in and intervened so I would not get an abortion. It was meant for my son to be born for such a time as this, and God has a great plan for him. Also, if I had gotten an abortion, I would not have any children. He is my only child. But most importantly, abortion goes against God's Word. It is the taking of a human life and the Lord kept me from going against His Word by preventing me from killing my child.

God is the Creator. He is the giver of life, and all life is precious to Him. The Bible shows that life begins at conception and that God fashioned us in our mother's womb. God called the Prophet Jeremiah and the Apostle Paul before they were born.

Jeremiah 1:5 - *Before I formed you in the womb I*

knew you; Before you were born I sanctified you; I ordained you a prophet to the nations.

Galatians 1:15 *- But when it pleased God, who separated me from my mother's womb and called [me] through His grace.*

When the voice of Mary, the mother of the Lord, was heard, John the Baptist leaped in his mother's womb.

Luke 1:44 *- For indeed, as soon as the voice of your greeting sounded in my ears, the babe leaped in my womb for joy.*

These scriptures reveal to us that children have spiritual identity in their mother's womb. Many women have had an abortion, but they never know and will never know who they had aborted. Who they had aborted could have been the next great prophet, pastor, missionary, President, scientist, doctor, singer, governor, congress person, or the next justice on the Supreme Court. He or she might have been someone who God was putting here to do something great that no one has ever done before. To end the life of an unborn child signifies that their life is not precious and important. But all humanity is precious and important to God.

Proof of wisdom is the actions it produces. At the age

of nineteen, Jesus gave me the wisdom to know that bringing men in and out of my life would affect my son and that I should not bring men in before my son, I should put my life on hold and be a good example as a mother to my son, and I should focus on him to create a clean, safe, stable home for him and not focus on a man. Jesus helped me keep to myself so that I would be a good witness to my son.

By the Lord's goodness and grace, I was able to do this. I had a male co-worker who also carpooled with me to work, and he had said to me more than once, "I like the way you are raising your son. I tell people about how you, as a single mother, are raising your son."

I have had another male friend tell me that he liked how I raised my son and that he wished the mother of his son would raise his son like I raise my son. I was surprised by both men's comments because I did not know that as men, they were noticing/observing how I treat my son, how I talk to my son, and how I represent myself before my son, but most importantly how my son was conducting himself. I did not know back then, that God had a hand on my son. Honestly, I feel that it was God who raised my son, and I only trained him.

A lot of women don't know that it is not good to

bring a lot of men in their home before their children. Women really do not know the true character of the men that they are just meeting and allowing in their life, home, and around their child/children and they do not think about how this would affect them. Some don't care because it's all about their needs, wants, and desires and not the child/children.

Another example comes to mind of a seven-year-old's tragic death. He was the youngest of three sons and the oldest was about fifteen years old. His mother started seeing a new man and moved her family in with him. The new man had a twelve-year-old son who began to molest the seven-year-old. When the mother found out about the molestation, she and her three sons moved out but did nothing about the molestation. She and her sons eventually moved back in with the boyfriend. Shortly thereafter, her seven-year-old son died of a heart attack. He died of a heart attack – do you hear me? This seven-year-old boy died of a heart attack because he was frightened. He was traumatized and was put back into a horrifying situation. He was so frightened that his heart stopped working. After this, the surviving two sons moved in with their grandmother to have a safe place to live.

Mothers don't realize that they are putting their children in dangerous situations until after the damage is done to their children. It's sad to say that after the damage is done, many mothers turn a blind eye to what is going on and continue to do damage or continue to allow damage to be done to their children. Do not think that the other two brothers' lives were not deeply affected by what had happened to their seven-year-old brother. Do not think that the brothers are not damaged by the tragic loss of their brother's life.

I know of several cases where girls have been molested by their mother's boyfriend and the mother knew of the molestation but chose to keep the boyfriend and blame the daughter for his actions. Some mothers have even put their daughters out of the house. These girls were damaged by the double pain and hurt that was inflicted upon them from the mother's boyfriend and by their own mother, who they looked to for protection.

Damaged children turn into damaged teens and damaged teens turn into damaged adults and damaged adults produce damaged children and the cycle continues. The mother's needs and wants for a man took top priority in the life of the mother of the seven-year-old boy. She did not create a safe and secure environment for her sons. Your children need to be in a safe, secure, protected environment and as mothers that should be your top priority – to provide this for them.

Mothers, I encourage you: please do not speak negatively to your children about their father, and do not bash him. That is the father of your children and whatever you may be feeling (which could be resentment, bitterness, hurt, rejection, or anger) is between you and the dad and not your children. Do not put them in the middle of that. Your children have nothing to do with that. They should not have to suffer because you feel some kind of way towards their dad. This affects them greatly. This affects the love and strong bond that could possibly be between them and their dad. This type of action gives the child/children a negative image about their dad. Let them love their dad and be with their dad, especially if their dad is trying to be with them.

Children need to be loved by their dad and should be free to love him back. Children should be able to talk about their dad in a loving way and not be in fear of being lashed out at by their mother if they say anything good about their dad. When you were lying down with him to create this child and you were loving on him, you were not putting him down or bashing him. But now that the relationship is over between you and you feel hurt, abandoned, alone, and rejected, you want to bash him. You want revenge. You want to hurt him because you are hurting. Many mothers, because of this hurt they are feeling, will inflict that hurt on their children by lashing out at them and saying all kinds of hurtful and harsh things to them.

We all have to forgive. I know you are thinking you can't do that because they did this or that to you, but the Word tells us:

Ephesians 4:31 - *Let all bitterness, wrath, anger, clamor, and evil speaking be put away from you, with all malice.*
4:32 - And be kind to one another, tenderhearted, forgiving one another, even as God in Christ forgave you.

It is important to forgive. The forgiveness is not for the person who hurt you. The forgiveness is for your benefit, so you can move forward with your life so you will not be stuck in the moment that the hurt was inflicted upon you by living it over and over and building up anger, resentment, and other feelings.

Matthew 6:15 - *But if you do not forgive men their trespasses, neither will your Father forgive your trespasses.*

The Word tells us to forgive others of their offenses and our Heavenly Father will also forgive us; but if we do not forgive others our Heavenly Father will not forgive us. It is very important that we walk in forgiveness.

The first step is to recognize that you have unforgiveness. You might wonder how to know if you have unforgiveness. If you have resentment, bitterness, anger, or are holding a grudge or being vindictive toward the person who inflicted the pain, you have unforgiveness.

Once we acknowledge this truth, we tell Jesus that we want change in our hearts, ask Jesus to change our hearts, ask the Lord to help us forgive him, and ask the Lord to give us a heart of forgiveness and mercy.

I know that your heart has been broken. That is why you are hurting. Ask Jesus to pick up the shattered pieces of your heart and put it back together again. Ask Him to take away the hurt and pain that you are feeling. He is waiting to help you, but you have to want to be helped. You have to make that choice and take the first step to be set free. It is important for you to do this both for your own benefit and for the benefit of your children.

Children are a gift from our Heavenly Father. Children are a heritage from God. Our children belong to God. They are our children only in a secondary sense. God brought His children into the world through us and entrusted them in our care to take care of them. He entrusted us to train His children. Children are on loan to us from Heaven. He made everything and He owns everything. The earth and everything in it belongs to the Lord.

1 Corinthians 10:26 - *for "the earth [is] the LORD's, and all its fullness."*

Proverbs 22:6 - *Train up a child in the way he should go, And when he is old he will not depart from it.*

Training our children means giving them a solid and strong foundation to start off in life. Remember the fairy tale story about the three little pigs? The first pig built his house with straw and the big bad wolf came and huffed and puffed and blew his house down. The second pig built his house with sticks and the big bad wolf blew his house down. But the third pig built his house with bricks and the big bad wolf huffed and puffed many times but could not blow his house down because the third pig's house was built on a solid strong brick foundation. It did not matter how many times the big bad wolf huffed and puffed, he could not blow the house down.

During their formative years, we want to give our

children a solid and strong foundation so that strong foundation will flow over into their teenage years and early adult life. They will not depart from it. When a child has a strong foundation, the parent's and children's lives will be much easier compared to a child's life that was not given a solid strong foundation.

We are responsible for training our children. The grandparents, aunts, or uncles are not responsible for training our children. Their input is greatly appreciated, but the responsibility belongs to the parents. If we don't train them, the state, the streets, gangs, television, and the schools will. A lot of schools are programing and grooming children in their formative years into immorality; things that are not of God's Kingdom but of satan's.

Training our children is our responsibility; we alone have the full responsibility of training them. We cannot push our responsibility onto someone else or let that be taken from us. We have to take the responsibility of training children seriously because we must give an account to God.

Hebrews 4:13 - *And there is no creature hidden from His sight, but all things [are] naked and open to the eyes of Him to whom we [must give] account.*

A couple of years ago in my prayer time, I thanked the Lord for the parents He gave me and thanked Him for how they raised me. I prayed this a lot. Then one day the Lord said to me, "I raised you," and immediately I thought about this Scipture:

Proverbs 22:6 - *Train up a child in the way he should go, And when he is old he will not depart from it.*

The scripture does not say raised it says train. So now I thank Him for raising me and I thank Him for my parents who trained me.

We are to be training our children in the way that they should go by giving them that strong foundation. We should train our children in the things of God. Train them to become fruitful in godly living. By doing so, our children will learn respect, they will have morals, values, integrity, and will follow God's direction and guidance. Failure to do so will lead our children down the wrong path – a path that leads to destruction.

It is very important how we, as parents, live our lives in front of our children. Children, in their formative years, are looking at our behavior imitating what they see us do. They are listening to what we are saying, and they will repeat what they hear. Children are like a sponge soaking up everything because they are in their learning stage.

Daughters imitate their mothers, and they usually turn out the way their mothers are in the way they dress, speak, and act. If a mother is messing with married men, then most likely that is what their daughter(s) will do. If a mother chases men, most likely their daughter(s) will do the same. If a mother is living her life on public assistance, then most likely their daughter(s) will too. If a mother uses profanity when talking to their daughter, most likely the daughter will use profanity when they talk to their mother and child/children. If a mother lashes out at her children, then the children will most likely lash out at their children. This is learned behavior and the parents are teaching them how to behave.

A woman I know who is now in her early thirties has no respect for her mother. She talks to her mother any way she wants to and has done some terrible things to her mother. So, I asked the mother what was going on and she said her daughter told her she hates her for the way she was treated as a child by the kids in the neighborhood because of her mother's lifestyle. The kids in the neighborhood knew and saw it and they made fun at her, especially on the school bus. So as a child, she was picked on and made fun of because of this, and this is affecting her life today. The mother's life has changed, she has given her life to the Lord, she even has asked her daughter for forgiveness, but her daughter will not forgive her.

Remember, forgiveness is a choice. So yes, the way we conduct ourselves and live out our lives in front of our children affects their lives. Our children will lose respect for us because we have lost respect for ourselves. They will start using profanity, telling us where to go and how to get there, disrespecting us, and not obeying us.

The Word tells us that:

Proverbs 18:21 *- Death and life [are] in the power of the tongue, And those who love it will eat its fruit.*

The tongue has power over life and death. A person's life largely reflects the fruit of their tongue what they speak out of their mouth. To speak life is to speak God's perspective on any issues of life. To speak death means to constantly speak negatively, to complain, or constantly speak in a defeated manner, like a victim or loser. Stop speaking death to your children.

You might ask, "How am I doing that?" You are doing that by speaking words like the following to them:

1. You are stupid, you are dumb.
2. You make me sick.
3. You will never amount to anything.
4. You're going to end up in gangs.
5. You are going to die in the streets.
6. You are going to end up in jail.
7. You are no good just like your dad.
8. You are nothing but a thief.
9. You can't do nothing right.
10 You are fat.
11 You are going to be a school dropout.
12 Etc.

This is speaking death to your child when you speak words like this to your children. You are speaking death into their life, you are putting a curse on them, you are giving what you are speaking permission to manifest in their life. I will repeat, you are giving what you are speaking permission to manifest in their lives.

Speak life to them, bless them, not curse them, by saying things like:

1. I love you.
2. You are a good son/daughter.
3. I am proud of you.
4. You do very well in school.
5. You are smart, you will go to college.

6. You have wisdom.
7. You will achieve much in life.
8. You are always there for your siblings, you are a good example to them.
9. I know that you will always choose to do the right thing.
10. You are a blessing to me, I am glad the Lord bless me with you.

These are examples of speaking life into their lives. You are blessing them. You are encouraging them. You are giving them hope. Even if their actions right now do not reflect this, still speak it; it will manifest in their lives where they will start producing the fruit that reflects what you have spoken.

The Word tells us in Romans 4:17 to call those things which do not exist as though they did. We can release the creative power of God's Word by believing it, even though we are facing challenging circumstances. Start decreeing and declaring the goodness of Jesus on your life and your children's lives.

The Word tells us:

Job 22:28 - *You will also declare a thing, And it will be established for you; So light will shine on your ways.*

Start decreeing and declaring:

1. In the mighty name of Jesus Christ of Nazareth, I decree and declare that (your child's name) will give their life to the Lord, they will be saved.

2. In the mighty name of Jesus Christ of Nazareth, I decree and declare that (your child's name) will excel in school.

3. In the mighty name of Jesus Christ of Nazareth, I decree and declare that (your child's name) will not be on drugs, in gangs, and in the streets.

Remember, death and life is in the power of the tongue. The tongue is very powerful. Our words are powerful. Satan tries and wants to keep us in the dark about the power of our words. He entices us to use our words for harm instead of hope, blessings, and life.

We cannot use our tongues (through our words) for profanity, harm, fussing, complaining, and speaking negatively to our children and other people. We must use our tongues (our words) to bless and encourage our children and declare and speak blessing upon them. As mothers, we are to do our best in taking care of God's precious ones.

I encourage you to give your children back to God and let Him raise them and you train them. When you are in doubt, ask Him for guidance and He will guide you according to His Word.

Chapter Six
The Root of Your Issues is Your Heart

If your life evidence displays what has been spoken in the previous chapters, know that the root of your issues(s) is your heart – the condition of your heart. What is in your heart?

1 Thessalonians 5:23 - *Now may the God of peace Himself sanctify you completely; and may your whole spirit, soul, and body be preserved blameless at the coming of our Lord Jesus Christ.*

Remember, Genesis 1:26- tells us that we were made in God's image.

Genesis 1:26 - *Then God said, "Let Us make man in Our image, according to Our likeness; let them have dominion over the fish of the sea, over the birds of the air, and over the cattle, over all the earth and over every creeping thing that creeps on the earth."*

And also:

John 4:24 - *God [is] Spirit, and those who worship Him must worship in spirit and truth.*

The spirit comes first so all humans are spirit-beings. And it says:

Genesis 2:7 *KJV - And the LORD God formed man [of] the dust of the ground, and breathed into his nostrils the breath of life; and man became a living soul.*

God formed man from the dust of the ground. Since our physical body is from the dust of the ground, our bodies are the same elements as the earth's elements. It is with our bodies that we are able to inhabit planet earth. Our soul is our mind, will, and emotions. We are a spirit being with a living soul in a shell of a body.

Matthew 22:37 - *Jesus said to him, "'You shall love the LORD your God with all your heart, with all your soul, and with all your mind.'*

22:38 - This is [the] first and great commandment.

22:39 - And [the] second [is] like it: 'You shall love your neighbor as yourself.'

Heart[12]: Intellect, awareness, mind, inner person, inner feelings, deepest thoughts, inner self.

Your soul is your mind, will, and emotions.

Mind[13]: The faculty of thought.

Our neighbor is another person regardless of nationality, gender, status, or age. Our neighbor is anyone who is in need. In the Book of Luke, Chapter 10, verses 25-37, Jesus tells us who our neighbor is through the Parable of the Good Samaritan. We are a neighbor if we show mercy to another person, no matter who they are or where they come from.

The heart is the seat of the soul. The heart is where your soul is located. Your soul is what needs to be saved. Your soul is the cause of all your sins. Remember the soul is your mind, will, and emotions.

1.   **Your mind**: This is your thought life, and sin starts in your mind. Satan speaks to your mind, telling you to do this, do that, telling you lies. He tells you to steal, commit adultery, fornicate, etc. God does not speak to your mind. He only speaks to your spirit.

---

[12] Word Wealth, Spirit-Filled Life Bible, NKJV
[13] Word Wealth, Spirit-Filled Life Bible, NKJV

2. **Your will**: We always want to do what we want to do, when we want to do it, and how we want to do it. We live in a Burger King and microwave society. We want it our way and we want it now. But we need to put down our will and pick up His will.

> ***Isaiah 55:8*** - *For My thoughts [are] not your thoughts, Nor [are] your ways My ways," says the LORD.*

3. **Your emotions**: Anger, rage, fear, hate, sorrow, hurt, jealousy, rejection etc.

> ***Mark 7:21*** - *For from within, out of the heart of men, proceed evil thoughts, adulteries, fornications, murders,*
>
> ***7:22*** - *thefts, covetousness, wickedness, deceit, lewdness, an evil eye, blasphemy, pride, foolishness.*
>
> ***7:23*** - *All these evil things come from within and defile a man.*

The heart is the central organ which conditions your activities. The heart is the center of your personality, the seat of your entire mental and moral activity which also contains your emotional elements. It is the seat of your feelings, desires, joy, pain, and love. It is also the center for your thoughts, understanding, and your will.

To sum it up, every choice, every decision, and everything you do flows from your heart. The condition of your heart is a true reflection of who you are, and your actions reflect what is in your heart. the Bible tells us:

Proverbs 27:19 - *As in water face [reflects] face, So a man's heart [reveals] the man.*

In today's society, I have seen women physically and verbally fighting women over a man. The majority of the time, it is the woman who is either married, engaged, or in a relationship with the man that is fighting other women. First of all, you are in a relationship with the man; you are not in a relationship with the woman. That woman did not force your husband, or your fiancé, or someone who you are dating into a sexual relationship. And if she did approach him first, then he should have been honest with her and said no I am married, no I am engaged, or no I am already dating someone. A lot of women really do not care if the man is married, engaged, or in a relationship; they still will consent to a sexual liaison. And a lot of times, men who are married, engaged, or in a relationship will lie and present themselves to women as being single. Still, it takes two consenting adults for anything sexual to happen and it is obvious that he, your man, consented to the act. So, your issue is with him and not the other woman.

A lot of women do go after the other woman and won't confront the man because they have a fear of losing him, they may have low self-esteem, they may feel that some attention from him is better than no attention; they may have a fear of being alone; maybe for financial reasons; maybe they have been married before and the first marriage did not work out and they don't want this marriage to fail; or maybe it's their first marriage and they don't want a failed marriage which ends in divorce. So, they put up with the emotional abuse, the lying, and the cheating.

Let's be honest, you know he will do it again and that is why you are going after the other woman trying to remove her. Don't think that when you go after the woman that the man won't do it again. Even if it is not with the same woman, he will do it again because he knows that you will attack her and not confront him so he will do it again. But most importantly, he will do it again because that is what is in his heart, and what is in the heart will reflect on the outside in his actions which is the lying, the cheating, and the abuse. Unless his heart changes, his actions will not change. And the same for you ladies – unless your heart changes, you will continue to physically and verbally fight women over a man.

As we talked about earlier in the book, transformation comes when your mind has been renewed and you come to believe and know your self-worth and you start realizing you deserve to be treated better than how you are being treated now. When you begin to value yourself, when you start having self-respect, and most of all when you begin to love yourself, you would not be in any relationship like that. Because if you truly love yourself, you would not let a male or a female treat you like that. And if you don't love yourself, how can you say you love Jesus, your children, or anyone.

Ladies, you are in relationships with satan's sons expecting a godly result. *News Flash*: it is not going to happen.

Godly results do not come from the sons of satan; godly results come from the sons of God. I am not saying that a son of God will not cheat/sin because many have backslidden, been tempted, and have entered back into sin. But they got convicted by the Holy Spirit, they repented, and turned back to God and have not gone that way again.

John 10:10 - *The thief does not come except to steal, and to kill, and to destroy. I have come that they* *may have life, and that they may have [it] more abundantly.*

Satan[14]: An opponent, the hater, the accuser, adversary, enemy, one who resists, obstructs, and hinders whatever is good.

This is saying what the thief, who is satan, comes to do:
1. Steal your joy.
2. Steal your happiness.
3. Steal your peace.
4. Steal your health.
5. Etc.

Satan, the thief, is a killer who comes to:
1. To kill you.
2. To kill your children.
3. To kill your loved ones.
4. To kill everything that is precious to you.
5. Etc.

Satan, the thief, is a destroyer who comes to:
1. Destroy your marriage.
2. Destroy your relationships.
3. Destroy your finances.
4. Destroy your home.

---

[14] Word Wealth, Spirit-Filled Life Bible, NKJV

5. Destroy your job.
6. Destroy your mind.
7. Etc.

Abundantly[15]: Superabundance, excessive, over-flowing, surplus, over and above, more than enough, extraordinary, above the ordinary, more than sufficient

On one side is God with goodness, life, and plenty of all that is necessary for life. On the other side is death, satan, the enemy of our souls who comes to rob us of God's blessings, to oppress our bodies through disease and accidents etc., and to destroy everything that we love and hold dear. Satan is the hate. He is all the more opposed to God, who is love.

The above scripture, John 10:10, tells us that satan came to do this. So, understand he is also using his sons and daughters and is operating through them (the unsaved) to do this. Just like God's sons and daughters (saved and Christ-like) represent Him and His Kingdom, satan's sons and daughters (the unsaved) represent him and his kingdom.

Our speech, our actions, our deeds, and what we are evidencing in our life shows who our father truly is

---

[15] Word Wealth, Spirit-Filled Life Bible, NKJV

and who we are truly serving. For example, satan will use that cheating man to tell you lies to justify why he is cheating. He may say things to you like, "You nag too much, you argue too much, you are not giving me what I need, you are not satisfying me, you are not making me happy, you are too fat, you are too small, you make me sick etc." Anything in an attempt to justify his sinful acts. A lot of you have bought into satan's lies, thinking to yourself things like, "If I do better in this area, if I dress provocatively, if I start doing this then he will stop etc." No, he will not stop, because that is who he is. That is what is in his heart. It is not you, it is satan using that man to destroy, kill, and steal, your joy, home, family, peace, and mind.

I was friends with a married couple and knew the husband to be a man who chased women. The wife was a very good wife to him. She cooked for him (and she definitely knew how to cook), she kept their house spotless (I never saw a dirty glass or dish in the sink and never saw anything out of place), she always looked very presentable, she had self-respect, she did not drink or smoke or use profanity, and she never stepped outside of her marriage. But yet, her husband cheated on her and that is what destroyed her marriage. After her marriage was destroyed, she started to drink heavily. You see, she did everything right, both domestically and morally, and he still cheated.

Let's all learn from this. Let's stop thinking it's our fault that he is cheating. It is what is in his heart; that is who he truly is.

Mark 7:21 - *For from within, out of the heart of men, proceed evil thoughts, adulteries, fornications, murders,*
7:22 -thefts, covetousness, wickedness, deceit, lewdness, an evil eye, blasphemy, pride, foolishness.

We talked earlier in the book about adultery, fornication, and lewdness. These come from the heart. The source of uncleanness, defilement, immorality, and evil actions. I have taught on immorality, and I am always hearing people say, "God knows my heart." But they say this to justify their sinful lifestyle and error. But what I say to that is this: your heart is the reason for your immorality and the reason why you are living your life in sin.

Jeremiah 17:9 - *The heart [is] deceitful above all [things], And desperately wicked; Who can know it?*
17:10 - I, the LORD, search the heart, [I] test the mind, Even to give every man according to his ways, According to the fruit of his doings.

The heart is more deceitful than anything else.

Immorality, harlotry, unclean acts, and other kinds of iniquity are a reflection of a sinful heart. Yes, God does know our hearts because God looks on the heart. He knows all human hearts. He does not overlook your sinful deeds. He does not and will not conform to our unclean lifestyle. He will not bow down to our worldly standards.

God knows what our motive or agenda for any act we show towards our neighbor, are you really loving your neighbor? Is it really an act of kindness or is there an agenda behind the act? He knows. So yes, God does know your heart; good or bad, He knows it.

The human heart reflects the person: a good person produces good things from the treasure of a good heart and an evil person produces evil things from the treasure of an evil heart. From out of the abundance of your heart, your mouth speaks. So, what we say and what we do flows from what is in our hearts.

Also, the Word says:

1 Peter 5:8 - *Be sober, be vigilant; because your adversary the devil walks about like a roaring lion, seeking whom he may devour.*

We have to take an assertive stance against the adversary, the devil. because of his mission, to steal, to kill, and to destroy. The above scripture tells us he walks about like a roaring lion seeking for anyone that he can devour. He knows that his time is short here on earth, so he is trying to take many people to hell with him.

This is from the Book of Job:

Job 1:7 - *And the LORD said to Satan, "From where do you come?" So Satan answered the LORD and said, "From going to and fro on the earth, and from walking back and forth on it."*

Satan is roaming through the earth, wandering here and there, looking for lives he can destroy, kill, and steal from.

Satan will truly destroy us if we let him. One way of letting him is having an unclean heart, by living a sinful life. If we have an unclean heart and are living our lives in sin, we have opened the door for him to come into our lives and control us.

I hear people say things like, "Why did God make me sick? Why did God take my family from me? Why did God make me homeless?" People want to put the blame for anything bad on God, but God is incapable of harming anyone. He will not bring devastation to you. As we stated before, Jesus said in John 10:10, I come to give you life and to give it more abundantly. Humans lie to you, but God does not lie to you.

Numbers 23:19 - *God [is] not a man, that He should lie, Nor a son of man, that He should repent. Has He said, and will He not do? Or has He spoken, and will He not make it good?*

He is incapable of lying, He is not a man that He should lie, nor a son of man that He should change His mind. Who are you going to put your trust in – God or satan?

1 John 4:16 - *And we have known and believed the love that God has for us. God is love, and he who abides in love abides in God, and God in him.*

Jesus is love and He extends mercy. Satan does not love you, he will never love you, and he will not extend mercy to you: he is here to take you, your family, and loved ones out.

Just like satan walks back and forth on the earth looking for whom he can devour, the Lord's eyes run to and fro throughout the whole earth looking for faithful hearts, hearts that are loyal to Him so He can show Himself strong in their lives.

2 Chronicles 16:9 - *For the eyes of the LORD run to*

and fro throughout the whole earth, to show Himself strong on behalf of [those] whose heart [is] loyal to Him. In this you have done foolishly; therefore from now on you shall have wars.

What He is saying is that those whose hearts are fully devoted to Him, He will bless. He is there for you and He is going to show up on your behalf. In other words, He's got your back. He is very faithful. He is loyal and trustworthy, and He sent His Son Jesus Christ to die on that cross for our sins. That is the love He has for us.

The human heart is the dwelling place of the Lord. Our most holy, omniscient Lord sees into your innermost being where all our decisions concerning Him are made. The Lord searches the minds and hearts, and He will give to each one according to what each person's deeds deserve.

Romans 2:6 - *who "will render to each one according to his deeds":*
2:7 - eternal life to those who by patient continuance in doing good seek for glory, honor, and immortality;
2:8 - but to those who are self-seeking and do not obey the truth, but obey unrighteousness-- indignation and wrath,

2:9 *- tribulation and anguish, on every soul of man who does evil, of the Jew first and also of the Greek;*

Unbelievers will be judged for their sins and believers will be judged for the good work they have done here on earth.

Proverbs 4:23 *- Keep your heart with all diligence, For out of it [spring] the issues of life.*
4:24 - Put away from you a deceitful mouth, And put perverse lips far from you.
4:25 - Let your eyes look straight ahead, And your eyelids look right before you.
4:26 -Ponder the path of your feet, And let all your ways be established.
4:27 - Do not turn to the right or the left; Remove your foot from evil.

Our hearts keep our values and protect our minds, emotions, and wills. Above everything else, we must guard our hearts because the adversary (the devil) is roaming the earth here and there looking for who he can devour.

We can guard our hearts by getting God's Word in our hearts. Ask the Lord to cleanse your heart. The goal is to keep our hearts with the greatest vigilance for out of it flows the issues of life; it is the source of life's consequences.

In my early days of being saved, I was attending a conference and I went into the office to register. When I entered the office, the person handling the registrations was waiting on someone. We were the only two people in the office but before she could finish registering the person in front of me, about four or five other people came in to register. So when she finally finished, she looked up and looked at someone who came in after me and said, "How can I help you?" I immediately thought to myself, "She knew I was next, she purposely waited on her next." Immediately in my heart I got offended. I did not say anything, but it was in my heart.

Later that day, the Lord told me to guard my heart and I knew what He was speaking to me about. I had to let that go; I could not let that linger in my heart. Satan was the one telling me, "She purposely did not wait on you. She knew you were next. She offended you." Remember, satan speaks to your mind. So, I learned from that to always guard my heart and to not open the door for satan to come in.

Our steps need to be guarded. By guarding our hearts, we will avoid a deceptive path. We should each ask the Lord to guide and direct our footsteps. Unless our hearts are transformed, our hearts will remain deceitful and wicked. When the condition of our hearts change, our lives will change. We can all ask God to cleanse our hearts. Asking God to create in us a clean heart and renew a standfast spirit (See Psalms 51:10).

Chapter Seven
Your Solution: Repentance Leads to Salvation

Confess: to declare openly by way of speaking out freely.

Repentance[16]: Is a decision that results in a change of mind which in turn leads to a change of purpose and action.

Salvation: Spiritual and eternal deliverance granted immediately by God to those who accept His conditions of repentance and faith in the Lord Jesus in whom alone it is to be obtained.

When the Holy Spirit first spoke to me in 1999, the very first thing He said to me was, "Going to church does not mean you are saved." I just knew the Holy Spirit was talking about someone else and not me, because I was brought up in the Church and was baptized at the age of five. I went up on my own, my parents did not encourage me to go up. My parents did

---

[16] Word Wealth, Spirit-Filled Life Bible, NKJV

not tell me that at the age of five, it is time for me to be baptized. I was sitting alone on the front pew in my church in my white dress, my parents were not sitting with me, when the invitation went out to the congregation for baptism, and I immediately went up.

As far back as I can remember, every Sunday we went to church, we had to go to church. There was no excuse for not going to church. I can't recall any Sunday when someone in my family stayed home from church. I can't remember one time that someone in my family was sick, and they could not attend church. A lot of times on Sunday when our church services were over, my parents took me to other church services. So, many Sundays I spent all day in church.

I just knew there was no way I was not saved; I did not drink, I didn't commit murder, I did not commit adultery, but I was fornicating, I did not smoke cigarettes, but I was smoking marijuana, I did not use profanity, I treated people decently, I didn't steal, and I was an honest person. I just knew I was saved because I was a good person and did good things. I got baptized at age five and remember being asked before baptism if I accepted Jesus as my Lord and Savior and answering yes. So at that point, I thought I was saved and always saved.

As I grew older, my lifestyle changed. I was living my life outside of God's ways. I was not living a righteous life before the Lord. I did not have a personal relationship with the Lord. I was not reading His Word. I did not know who He really was; I knew of Him, but I did not truly know Him. To know Him is to experience Him.

When the Lord said this to me, I had to make a choice. It was either the man I was in a relationship with or Jesus. And I choose Jesus. I got out of the relationship that I was in, I stopped fornicating, I confessed my sins, and I gave my life totally to the Lord. I turned away from everything in my life that was not in alignment with His Word, and I became born again.

So, I am saying to you what the Holy Spirit said to me: just because you go to church faithfully every Sunday does not guarantee that you are saved.

Ladies, you say you are saved, what are you saved from? Because a lot of you are exhibiting all the principles of the world and not the principles of Jesus. Just because you say you are a Christian does not mean that you are a Christian. Being a Christian means being Christ-like and becoming more and more like Christ.

Christianity is not a religion, it is living a life in Christ. Are you Christ-like or are you satan-like? Do you represent God's Kingdom, or do you represent satan's kingdom? If you say you are a Christian, but your lifestyle exhibits what has been spoken in the previous chapters, then are you really saved?

The scripture tells us "You will know them by their fruits." (Matthew 7:16.) Fruits is your life-style, character, your actions. So, whose fruits are you exhibiting in your life? I encourage you to really examine your life and if you are honest with yourself and really recognize yourself as exhibiting what was spoken of in the previous chapters, I encourage you to confess your sins, repent of your sins, turn from everything that goes against God's Word, and receive Jesus Christ as your Lord and Savior.

If you have given your life to the Lord but have entered back into sin, turn back in repentance so that your relationship with Him will be restored. Rededicate your life to the Lord.

If you have never given your life to the Lord, confess your sins to the Lord, receive Jesus as your Lord and Savior and get a personal relationship with Him. Ask Him to deliver you from the bondage of sin. Dedicate your life to Him, forgetting the attractions of the world, and follow Jesus our Savior.

1 John 1:9 *- If we confess our sins, He is faithful and just to forgive us [our] sins and to cleanse us from all unrighteousness.*

Confessing your sins allows you to receive the Lord's forgiveness and cleansing. Know that He is trustworthy and just, trust Him to forgive you, cleanse and purify you from wrongdoing.

The scripture says:

Romans 10:9 *- that if you confess with your mouth the Lord Jesus and believe in your heart that God has raised Him from the dead, you will be saved.*
10:10 *- For with the heart one believes unto righteousness, and with the mouth confession is made unto salvation.*

If you acknowledge publicly with your mouth that Jesus is Lord and trust in your heart that God raised Him from the dead, you will be saved. Verbal confession declares, confirms, and seals the belief in your heart. With the heart one goes on trusting.

Jesus gave His life for us. He lived a sinless life, a perfect life without sin. He died for our sins. He shed His blood for us. We have redemption through His blood, and the forgiveness of our sins which allows us to draw closer to God.

Enter into a right relationship with God. As you give yourself totally to Jesus, He gives His total self to you.

Matthew 6:33 - *But seek first the kingdom of God and His righteousness, and all these things shall be added to you.*

As you seek first the Kingdom of God and His righteousness, He has promised us all these things shall be added to us. But most importantly you will have eternal life. Isn't this worth having?

Set your thinking and affections on Jesus Christ and build your relationship with Him. Do not allow worldly pursuits to draw you away from Him. Do not be conformed to this world.

Let us take a moment now and ask God in prayer to cleanse us, renew our minds, and set us on a path to being virtuous and temperate women.

Abba Father, I ask that You forgive me for all of my sins, knowing and unknowing in deeds, thoughts, action and speech. Lord, I ask that You come into my life as my Lord and Savior and teach me Your ways. Lord, cleanse me by the blood of Jesus Christ. Lord, direct and guide my footsteps and put my feet on the path to become a virtuous and temperate woman. Lord, have mercy on me and help me to walk in Your ways. Father, deliver me from the power of darkness and convey me into the kingdom of the Son of Your love.

Change me Lord, purify my heart, and make me more like You. Father, give me a new heart and put a new Spirit within me, take the heart of stone out of my flesh and give me a heart of flesh. Give me a hunger and thirst for Your Word, for Your righteousness, for the things of You, and fill that hunger and thirst. Lord, I ask that You renew my mind, and give me Your wisdom and understanding, that I may have the mind of Christ. Father, help me to be a doer of the Word and not a hearer only. Father, I ask that You send Spiritual laborers across my path to help me along my journey. Lord, give me a heart of forgiveness, and keep me from evil. Lord, please set me free. Do a good work in and through me. In Jesus mighty name. Amen.

I encourage you to open up the door and let Jesus into your heart and let Him do a new thing in your life. May mercy, peace, and love be multiplied to you.

Revelation 1:8 - *I am the Alpha and the Omega, [the] Beginning and [the] End," says the Lord, "who is and who was and who is to come, the Almighty.*

Acknowledgements

I want to thank my parents, the late Alphonso Lagustus Jackson Sr, and late Lonia Mae Jackson, who trained my two brothers and me up in the ways of the Lord, and who instilled in us morals, integrity, and self-respect, including to treat other people with respect.

I praise and thank my Heavenly Father who called me in my mother's womb and raised me up in His ways and His standards so I can be used for His Kingdom work.

I also thank the Lord for guiding and directing my footsteps to Calvary Pentecostal Tabernacle. I thank Pastor Jane Lowder, Director of CPT, Pastor Debbie Garland and the many Pastors and Ministers who have preached and taught at CPT and imparted into my life.

The Story of How this Book Came to Be

In 2005, I was attending a women's conference at CPT in Ashland, Virginia. I was prayed over by a pastor from New Jersey, and she said, "You are a woman of virtue, write the book." I was thinking, "I am not a writer, I never even thought of writing a book, and I do not know what the book should be about." Twice I started writing this book, only to write a few pages, because I thought, "This is not it, this is not the subject I am supposed to write about," and I would stop writing.

In June 2021, I was attending summer services at CPT and brother Paul Aloo, from New York, said to me, "The Lord says you have a book in you, so write it." Then he said, "I heard the Spirit say, 'Book on your heart.'" In the last few years, I have told several women (and maybe one or two men) that if I ever get a chance to talk to women, I will teach them about morals and how they should conduct themselves. It saddens me to see how women are conducting and displaying themselves these days. This is what I have had on my heart: a burden for women.

So, I pondered on what the minister said to me, and it came back to my spirit what the Pastor had said to me in 2005 at the Women's Conference. I re-read what she had said, and then it came to me what I was to write about. She had said to me, "You are **a woman of virtue**, write the book."

Once again, in July 2021 while attending summer service at CPT, I had just met my roommate and as soon as we introduced ourselves to one another, the next thing out of her mouth was, "I hope you don't take this the wrong way, but I hope you will be obedient to God and write the book." I was shocked and I told her that I had just been here in June when brother Paul Aloo told me, "There is a book in you, write the book;" and now she was confirming what was revealed to him. Then she said, "Titus 2 woman." I told her, "I am going to write the book." Then we prayed in agreement for the birthing of this book.

2 Corinthians 13:1[17] - This will be the third time I am coming to you. By the mouth of two or three witnesses every word should be established.

Three different people were witnesses to what the Lord wanted me to do. The matter was established; I

---

[17] The Spirit-Filled Life Bible, NKJV

have heard from the Lord three times on writing the book and I knew it was time for me to be obedient. Fear had set in me, because my Abba Father first spoke to me on writing the book in 2005, then again in June 2021, and then again in July 2021, so I was thinking that He may not be pleased with me because I had not written the book yet. I repented and asked the Lord to forgive me for not being obedient to Him back in 2005. I committed to moving forth in obedience, and to start writing the book. So, 17 years later, I have finally been obedient to the Lord and have written this book. I pray it is a blessing to all who read it.

About the Author

Janice Mae Jackson (pronounced Jan-eece) lives in in the Maryland, Washington D.C. and Virginia area of the United States. She is a minister of the gospel, and the Pastor and leader of Go Ye Forth Ministry. She pastors and leads people to Christ by preaching the gospel, teaching the Bible, and training disciples to Go Ye Forth in fulfillment of the Great Commission. God has also sent her to minister in the nations, particularly to women and children in need of her loving care and exhortation.

Go Ye Forth Ministry
12138 Central Avenue, Suite 553
Mitchellville, Maryland 20721
janice@goyeforthministry.org

About Manifest Publications

Manifest Publications is the publishing division of Manifest International, LLC. Our objective is to help like-minded ministries and writers produce and distribute materials which proclaim Jesus Christ to all the world and equip the global Church for unity and maturity.

MANIFEST
PUBLICATIONS

www.manifestinternational.com